REVERSING SELF- DESTRUCTIVE PATTERNS

A product of
The Chapel of the Air

MULT

Portland,

Unless otherwise indicated, Scripture references are from the Holy Bible: New International Version, copyright 1973, 1978, 1984 by the International Bible Society. Used by permission of Zondervan Bible Publishers.

Verses marked (TLB) are from The Living Bible, © 1971 owned by assignment by Illinois Regional Bank N.A. (as trustee). Used by permission of Tyndale House Publishers, Inc., Wheaton, Ill. 60189. All rights reserved.

Edited by Steve Halliday
Cover design by Durand Demlow
Written by Steve Bell, David Mains, and Marian Oliver, assisted by Randy Petersen.

REVERSING SELF-DESTRUCTIVE PATTERNS
© 1990 by The Chapel of the Air
Published by Multnomah Press
10209 SE Division
Portland, Oregon 97266

Multnomah Press is a ministry of Multnomah School of the Bible, 8435 N.E. Glisan Street, Portland, Oregon 97220.

Printed in the United States of America

ISBN 0-88070-404-7

90 91 92 93 94 95 - 6 5 4 3 2

Dedicated to
Steve Halliday,
whose encouragement and help
in this project were invaluable.

Part 1

Reversing Self-Destructive Patterns

The panther is like a leopard,
Except it hasn't been peppered.
Should you behold a panther crouch,
Prepare to say Ouch.
Better yet, if called by a panther,
Don't anther.[1]

Long before Ogden Nash dreamed up his whimsical rhyme, a man named Peter used the same sort of logic to warn his friends about another beast. But the creature Peter had in mind was infinitely more dangerous than a panther:

Be careful—watch out for attacks from Satan, your great enemy. He prowls around like a hungry, roaring lion, looking for some victim to tear apart. Stand firm when he attacks. Trust the Lord . . . (1 Peter 5:8, 9a, TLB).

Everyone, at some time, confronts this hungry lion—male/female, young/old, healthy/sick, rich/poor, Christian/non-Christian, black, white, Hispanic, Oriental. His avowed purpose is to destroy anyone he can sink his fangs into. Most often his strategy calls for use of a devastating weapon called . . . *temptation*.

Temptation escapes no one. If you're alive, you're going to be tempted. Face it. Still, it's not really the temptation that's the problem. No, it's when we *give in* to those temptations that we run headlong into trouble. Far too often, giving in to temptation leads to self-destructive habits that ultimately destroy our happiness, our relationships, even our very lives.

This book is about reversing self-destructive patterns. It's about beating the enemy and sending him away licked. And the strategy it contains already has proven effective for many:

> A minister, upset by the negative attitude of someone in his congregation, fell into the routine of bad-mouthing his critic. But the pastor caught his destructive habit, battled it, and in seven short weeks completely reversed the pattern.

> A woman grew bitter over a misunderstanding with a co-worker. But the Holy Spirit used a Scripture verse to challenge her about her critical spirit. Memorizing that verse helped bring healing to her life before the bitterness became destructive.

What temptations repeatedly trouble you? It's important to be specific in answering such a question. You won't learn to reverse self-destructive patterns if you can't identify them by name. Most people are conscious of several destructive patterns in their lives, so that's why the question was asked in the plural. It's also true that we're often blind to some of our most serious flaws.

Satan wants to destroy us

Have you ever wondered why the self-destructive habits that plague us are often so hard to eradicate?

One major reason can be spelled out in five letters: S-a-t-a-n. Satan is an evil, malicious, powerful spirit who will do anything he can to send us plunging over the brink. That's why we must be careful. We must watch out for his attacks.

The truth is, however, that Satan doesn't initially appear to be so malevolent. Often he seems most empathetic. When no one else understands, he does. And he gives us the very excuses we need to give in to his enticing suggestions.

"Think of the pressure you're under," he whispers. Or, "You know in a showdown you can beat this problem, so why be so concerned?" Or, "Other people wouldn't even consider this a sin. They'd say, 'Why be bothered by things like that? You ought to hear what troubles me!' " Or, "You know a Christian leader who has that very same problem. Everybody knows about it and they excuse him."

At a time of pressure in your life, how nice it is to have someone who seems to understand. But what this enemy doesn't say is that as soon as you give in to the temptation, his tune changes. In an instant he attacks. "You knew that was wrong before you did it! In the Sunday school lesson you taught last week, you told your students that God doesn't tolerate this kind of behavior. Why don't you just give up and quit trying to be a Christian?" Or, "I heard you tell God that if he would forgive you, you would never, ever do that again. You cried when he forgave you. You expect him just to forgive you now as though you hadn't made that promise?" Or, "I would stay away from God for a while if I were you. He doesn't like it when people do what you just did. Put a little distance between what's happened and the next time you get with him." Or,

"You know what you are? A big hypocrite! You say one thing and live another. There's nothing worse in all the world than a hypocrite."

Suddenly, Satan's true character is revealed. He never was a friend. All along he wanted to destroy you.

Don't be deceived: The more you listen to him, the more you're headed for trouble!

Jesus has always known Satan's true character. Long before Myers and Briggs developed their personality type indicator, Jesus labeled the devil a liar and a murderer. Here is Jesus' evaluation:

> [Satan] was a murderer from the beginning, not holding to the truth, for there is no truth in him. When he lies, he speaks his native language, for he is a liar and the father of lies (John 8:44b).

Who likes liars? Who is attracted to murderers? Most people are uncomfortable around those with a reputation for not telling the truth. And would you welcome a murderer into your home?

Thieves and murderers only want to harm you. Always remember Satan's deadly designs, even though he masquerades as someone who wants only what's good for you.

We have an opportunity to overcome

In our effort to reverse self-destructive patterns, we must understand one thing at the outset: Temptation in itself is not necessarily bad. If we could eliminate every temptation from our lives, we would probably forgo all opportunities for spiritual growth. Temptation may result in defeat, but it also provides the occasion to overcome.

Peter writes, "Stand firm when he attacks."

This book claims that fifty days can bring about a dramatic change in your life for the good. In fifty days you can reverse a self-destructive pattern. That's an exciting possibility.

Why fifty days? Because we're not interested in just gaining a victory here and there. We want to see the enemy soundly beaten. We want to establish new habit patterns, and in fifty days that can be done.

We know of a business executive who got hooked on pornographic magazines. Soon, the habit all but choked out his joy of living. Andrew was in despair and finally realized his only hope was to take definite measures against the problem. Today he testifies to a dramatic change. In fifty days, with help from Scripture and a concerned friend, he was able to reverse his self-destructive pattern. He maintains a healthy respect for the temptation, but it is no longer his master.

Did you know it is as difficult to break a good habit as it is a bad habit? That's true! If you can establish a winning routine for fifty days, there is every reason to believe that you will be able to continue that good habit on Day 51, Day 52, and thereafter.

Such a thought should fill you with hope!

Imagine what it would be like to no longer fall prey to the self-destructive patterns that trouble you. If you gained mastery over them, what advantages would be yours? For some people it would mean saving money; others would find marked improvement in their self-image. In many situations, victory would lead to a closer relationship with God. Some would see healing come to their family life.

Take a few moments right now to write down five positive improvements you would experience if you were to reverse a particular self-destructive pattern. If you could change defeat to victory in one area of temptation where currently you are still a victim, what would be the personal benefits?

1.

2.

3.

4.

5.

Those five items sure look good, don't they? Listen—if you want to see them happen, you need a plan. That's what this book provides. It's small, but powerful! It's a guide you can trust. Follow it precisely. Though there is room for varying personalities and traits, don't move away from the book's basic guidelines.

You will also need a friend. Without a friend to help, this venture will be severely limited. You'll need to find a spiritually sensitive friend who will ask how you're doing. You'll want a friend who will make sure you stick with what you've set out to do. You don't necessarily have to divulge what the problem is that you're trying to overcome, but you should say to your friend, "I'm trying to reverse a self-destructive pattern. I'm coming into this project with great seriousness. Would you please ask me how I'm doing? Contact me at least once a week. You have my permission to get after me if I seem to be slacking off."

Christ promises his help

You might have a question at this point. Is this merely a self-improvement program? Is it only a matter of individual determination?

The answer is a decided *no*.

As aware as you are of the enemy, you should be even more aware of the Lord's presence. From the very beginning, we want to involve him in what is to take place.

Peter writes, "Trust the Lord."

Begin now to ask the Lord which temptation he would have you work on. Don't just choose one on your own. Undergird your choice with prayer.

Also, you need to ask the Lord which friend you could ask to check on your progress. Perhaps he'll bring someone to mind you've never even considered. Begin now to pray about that matter as well.

A Christian employer needed someone to ask him daily about how he was doing in an unnamed area where he struggled. After prayer, he decided to ask one of his employees (also a Christian) if he would be willing to check on his progress. What could have been an awkward situation turned out to be mutually beneficial. "I'll do it," his worker responded, "if you'll do the same thing for me." I'm happy to report that both made marked improvement.

At the end of each day in this fifty-day enterprise, you will ask Jesus to grade you on your progress. That will be explained more fully in the second section of this book. Remember that you won't be measuring yourself against perfection. Rather, you will say to the Lord, "If you evaluated me today on how well I did in resisting my targeted temptation, what grade would you give me?" You'll find that Jesus is probably more lenient than you are yourself! There will be times when you sense he gives you a higher grade just because he knows you're going through a stressful time. You're struggling, but he sees you're making a great effort. Sometimes you will have to guess what grade Jesus would give you. Even so, the exercise will prove helpful.

Another great help in overcoming self-destructive patterns is to borrow a practice of Jesus himself. We want to adopt Christ's emphasis on Scripture memory. Remember how Jesus quoted Scripture when he was tempted by Satan in the wilderness? (You can read about that in Matthew 4:1-11.) For Weeks 1, 3, 5, and 7 of this exercise, we have chosen a Scripture for you to memorize. For example, during Week 1 you are to memorize 1 Corinthians 10:13:

> No temptation has seized you except what is common to man. And God is faithful; he will not let you be tempted beyond what you can bear. But when you are tempted, he will also provide a way out so that you can stand up under it.

This passage reminds us that we're not alone in our struggles. What a comfort! Down through the years, many believers have wrestled with the identical problems that haunt us. God made it possible for them to overcome. He will prove himself faithful to us as well.

During Weeks 2, 4, and 6, you will choose a Scripture on your own. To help you, we have included a whole section of passages that deal with sins that commonly trouble us. We haven't tried to cover every possible sin, nor under each category have we tried to include all the Scripture verses that (if memorized) would prove helpful. But our list of sins and suggested verses to memorize should get you on a healing track. There's also opportunity for you to choose a favorite verse that we didn't include. This is one area where you can express your personal preference.

At the beginning of that section of Bible verses you'll find tips for memorizing Scripture. Make use of them!

The road may be rocky

There will be times when you blow it. Does that mean it's all over for you? No way! Ask Christ to forgive you for what you've done. Like the psalmist, pray that God will return to you the joy of his salvation (Psalm 51:12).

Unfortunately, more people know about confession than actually practice it. Don't let that be the case with you during these fifty days. No one will make it through the entire exercise without being severely tested. The enemy doesn't give up ground without a fight! Remember that a lost battle doesn't mean the war can't be won. Let your failures motivate you to become even more diligent in achieving victory.

Long-established sins like workaholism don't get resolved instantly. Over-scheduling sometimes takes months—or even years—to correct. A businesswoman friend admits that it takes awhile to get used to saying, "I'm sorry; I can't do that. I already have too much on my plate!" But she says that making a mistake and learning from it is not the same as repeating the same mistake time and again.

When do you start? Again, that's an opportunity for you to express your individuality. You can choose whatever day you want as Day 1 of these fifty special days. After you have prayerfully sensed what self-destructive pattern Christ would have you work on and you know which friend you'll ask to help you, make Day 1 the date your friend agrees to ask how things are going for you.

Part 2 of this book is the Game Plan. Read it carefully. It's not complicated, but it is important. Don't pick and choose what you want to do. For example, don't say, "I'll mark the daily chart but I don't think I'll memorize the weekly Scriptures." This plan has been carefully crafted, so stick with it—trust us.

After Weeks 2, 4, and 6, you'll find specific guidelines to help you analyze the charting process you began on Day 1. The exercises are self-explanatory. You will find them helpful.

A second set of charts and guidelines for interpretation also has been included in this book. It serves either of two purposes:

1. It gives you the opportunity to continue your work on reversing a self-destructive habit if you're not satisfied with your progress in the first fifty days.

2. You can choose another self-destructive behavior, and with your just-completed positive experience under your belt, see rapid spiritual growth in another area.

If you'd like to continue this venture for other fifty-day periods, feel free to copy the charts and accompanying questions.

An example from Scripture

A well-loved story of Daniel is found in chapter 6 of the Old Testament book that bears his name. It tells of the respect King Darius had for Daniel, and how the enemies of this righteous man looked for an opportunity to destroy him.

They tricked Darius into proclaiming that no petition could be made of anyone save the king for a period of thirty days. Unaware of their true intent, Darius signed the edict, thus prohibiting Daniel from praying to his God for an entire month. If Daniel disobeyed, he risked being tossed into the royal den of lions.

What temptations do you suppose Daniel might have struggled with at this time? To give in to fear? To stop praying? To become bitter and to try avenging himself on his tormenters?

Imagine what the enemy might have said to him: "Thirty days are over in no time. Just lay low for a while." "Pray in secret. Who will know?" "People like you are needed in leadership. What good will result if you're killed?"

But Daniel knew Satan was not a true friend. Despite the king's edict, he continued his regular pattern of prayer.

Satan ached to destroy Daniel. No doubt he whispered to the grizzled old prophet, "With such an illustrious career, how could anything improve your record?" But Daniel apparently saw this incident as an opportunity to seize yet another great victory. He didn't know it, but he was about to embark on the most thrilling episode of his life. Though he was an old man when it happened, this was the event that people would associate with his name for generations to come.

Would God see him through? Would he be there, present, during Daniel's time of severe testing?

You know the story. Daniel spent all night in a den of ferocious beasts that normally would have ripped him apart. But their mouths were shut! God saw to that. The Lord proved faithful to his servant.

Ah, you think, *that's great for Daniel. But if they threw me in a den of lions, I'd be lunch meat in two seconds.* You may be partly right. The truth is, many Christians have been murdered for their faith. But that doesn't mean the Lord was any less present! Often, a martyr's last words have testified to a special awareness of God, a deep sense that the Lord was present even through these most desperate of times.

What does that mean to you? It means that the truth of what we're suggesting is not invalidated. Christ is still with us, and he still brings us through victoriously.

Having said that, we want you to be aware that you *are* in a lion's den. Let Peter remind you again.

> Be careful—watch out for attacks from Satan, your great enemy. He prowls around like a hungry, roaring lion, looking for some victim to tear apart. Stand firm when he attacks. Trust the Lord . . . (TLB).

Your great enemy wants to destroy you through the destructive pattern you're thinking about even now. But you have an opportunity to reverse that pattern, to defeat Satan, to rejoice in the hope that through Christ things can be marvelously different. Christ is the one who puts that hope in your heart. And he says, "I will be with you in everything that takes place, even during the next fifty days when the roaring lion growls. Trust me! Experience a great victory!"

Are you ready to trust him? Are you eager to whip a self-destructive pattern that's had you in its grip for too long? If so, you're all set to begin this powerful fifty-day program that could well change—forever!—the way you live.

Let's get started!

Part 2
The Game Plan

1. Identify a self-destructive pattern.

What are some temptations that continually trouble you? It may be wise not to start with your most difficult temptation the first time you do this fifty-day exercise. Instead, ask the Holy Spirit to help you pinpoint a simpler behavior pattern he wants to change in you. The next time, after you've gotten some practice, you'll be prepared to confront a bigger temptation. If you feel comfortable doing so, write on this line the self-destructive pattern you will be seeking to reverse during these fifty days:

_____

On page 10, you listed some personal benefits you would enjoy if you could resist a particular temptation. Now think about the self-destructive pattern you will be working on for the next fifty days. What will be the advantages of reversing this habit?

1.

2.

3.

4.

5.

2. Chart your behavior.

Each day, ask Jesus how he would rate your progress on a scale of 1 to 10 (10 means you are successfully overcoming the temptation and saying no to this self-destructive behavior). Then mark that point on the chart on page 22. There is a vertical line for each day; put a dot at the proper 1-10 level. As you connect the dots, you will see a pattern emerge. If you don't encounter your temptation, just skip that day on your chart. You can still connect the dots.

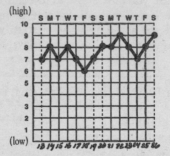

It's helpful to picture what victory over your self-destructive pattern will be like. For example, if you're fighting the problem of workaholism, you could set some goals like this: (1) Leave the office by 6 P.M. (2) Take half an hour to relax every night. (3) Don't open your briefcase at home in the evening until you've spent quality time with your family. What specific behaviors might mark your day when Jesus gives you a rating of 10?

_____

_____

_____

3. Analyze the pattern.

Special questions are included to help you interpret your chart after Weeks 2, 4, and 6 (see pages 25-33). You will be analyzing not only the timing of any sudden falls, but also the surrounding circumstances, who you were with, and so on.

4. Plan new behavior strategies.

You will use your analysis to plan new ways of living that should help you say no to this temptation more successfully. For instance, Jack is trying to change a pattern of insulting his wife. He discovers that he's especially nasty to her after he's been around his old buddy Frank. One way Jack can start to overcome his sin is to spend less time with Frank. Not all strategies will be that simple, but you should find specific ways to plan for improvement.

5. Memorize Scripture.

During the course of these fifty days, we suggest four passages that you will find especially helpful as you encounter temptation. They're listed under the "Weekly Checkpoints" on pages 23-24. Memorize these verses. Arm yourself with them. Use them. If you need help in how to go about memorizing verses, see the suggestions listed on pages 57-59.

We also ask you to find and memorize three short passages that relate specifically to your particular self-destructive pattern. If you want suggestions, Part 3 of this book lists verses on thirty common temptations. Note the verses you choose on the "Weekly Checkpoints" page.

6. *Tell someone that you're doing this exercise.*

It's always best if you can be completely honest, but it's not absolutely necessary to reveal the specific temptation you're confronting. At least tell the person that you're working on a problem area and would like him or her to check on your progress.

Remember: As you seek to imitate Christ, "it is God who works in you to will and to act according to his good purpose" (Philippians 2:13).

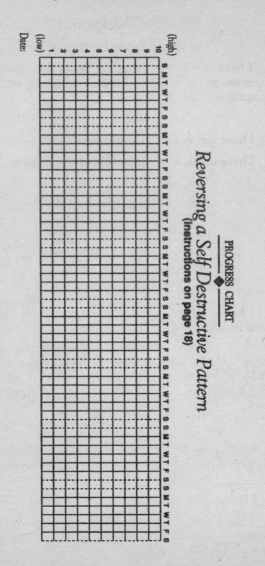

PROGRESS CHART

Reversing a Self Destructive Pattern
(Instructions on page 18)

Date:
(low)
(high)

Weekly Checkpoints

Preparation Step to Get Started

__ I have told a friend that I'm doing this fifty-day exercise, and I've asked him/her to check on my progress each week.

Week 1

__ I have memorized 1 Corinthians 10:13.

__ I have talked to my friend about my progress.

Week 2

__ I have chosen a Scripture to memorize related to my particular self-destructive pattern. The Scripture is _____.

__ I have memorized the Scripture I selected.

__ I have updated my friend on my progress this week.

__ I have completed the chart interpretation questions on pages 25-28.

Week 3

__ I have memorized Genesis 4:7.

__ I have updated my friend on my progress this week.

Week 4

__ I have chosen a Scripture to memorize related to my particular self-destructive pattern. The Scripture is _____.

__ I have memorized the Scripture I selected.

__ I have updated my friend on my progress this week.

__ I have completed the chart interpretation questions on pages 29-31.

Week 5

__ I have memorized Hebrews 4:15, 16.

__ I have updated my friend on my progress this week.

Week 6

__ I have chosen a Scripture to memorize related to my particular self-destructive pattern. The Scripture is _____.

__ I have memorized the Scripture I selected.

__ I have updated my friend on my progress this week.

__ I have completed the chart interpretation questions on pages 32-33.

Week 7

__ I have memorized Philippians 4:8.

__ I have updated my friend on my progress this week.

__ I have followed the suggestions on page 34 to bring closure to this fifty-day exercise.

Chart Interpretation
After Week 2

Look at the chart you've kept over the last two weeks (page 22). Maybe you're extremely pleased with your progress—that's great!

Now it's time to interpret your graph. Here arc a few examples.

If your chart looks like this, you do well on the weekends but have trouble during the week:

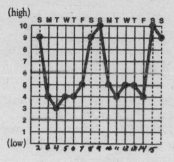

In contrast, if your chart looks like this, your trouble spots occur on the weekends:

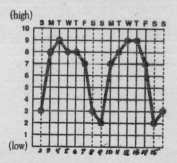

Perhaps you memorized the Scripture for the first week but let the second week's memory work slide. That may have affected your progress so that your chart looks like this:

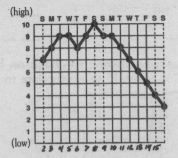

Maybe you were doing very well until, suddenly and unexpectedly, something tripped you. You thought, *If I can't get a perfect score, I might as well give up.* Your defeat lasted several days. If that's the case, your chart looks like this:

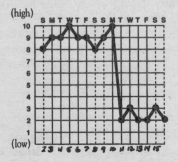

Whatever your chart looks like, this may be the first time you've ever seen your response to this temptation actually pictured before your eyes. Ask the Lord to help you interpret your graph. You may be pleased; you may be disturbed.

This is what my chart tells me about my progress in reversing my self-destructive pattern:

_____

_____

I have asked someone to check on how I'm doing. I think it would be appropriate to ask that person to pray for me as well.

__ Yes   __ No

If your chart shows a sudden upsurge or downturn, think back through the events of those days. Were there certain people you spent time with who may have affected your behavior in positive or negative ways?

These people affected my progress. Here's how:

_____

_____

These circumstances or events affected my behavior (being away from home, pressure at work, TV programs, staying up late, being sick, etc.):

_____

_____

What can you do to avoid yielding to your temptation the next time a troublesome situation arises?

_____

_____

Here's the positive coping technique I'm planning now to replace my self-destructive response:

_____

_____

Review the benefits of being free from your self-destructive pattern that you listed on page 17. Now take time to pray about it. Ask God to forgive you for your failures. Thank him for your victories. Ask him to help you implement the strategies you've worked out. And praise him for his patience and unconditional love.

(Note: If your scores are consistently below 4, you may need to go to someone for help. Again, you could ask a spiritually minded friend to hold you accountable. Or, you might talk to a minister or Christian counselor.)

Chart Interpretation
After Week 4

Now that you've charted your progress for four weeks, you're gaining more and more perspective on reversing your self-destructive pattern. So this is a good time to stop and evaluate again.

Remember the difference between temptation and sin? As we said in the introduction, temptation in itself is not bad. Because you're currently battling a self-destructive pattern, you may find that you're being tempted more often than usual. But don't lose sight of your goal. You should be charting only your *response* to temptation.

What does your chart look like (page 22)? Do you see an upward or downward slope, or a straight horizontal line? Have you reached a plateau?

The overall pattern of my chart is _____.

Is there a specific day of the week that seems to present a special problem for me? This might be the reason:

__ It's payday.

__ I always watch a certain TV program.

__ I usually see _____ (name of person).

Other: _____.

This is how I would describe my feelings about overcoming my self-destructive pattern:

__ Determined

__ Still trying

__ Backing off

__ Ambivalent

__ I'm not sure I feel committed to mastering my self-destructive pattern. This is what's holding me back:

_____

_____

__ I could really use a boost to improve my progress. Here's what I need:

_____

_____

I am continuing to memorize Scripture.

__ Yes __ No

If no, here's the reason:

_____

It's possible that since the beginning of this exercise, you've received some disturbing news or experienced added tension in your life. Or it could be that you've worked so hard to overcome temptation that the matter has become obsessive. In either case, you may need to relax and let go of this venture for awhile. That's okay. Decide whether this is a healthy exercise for you to continue at this time.

__ Yes, I plan to continue this exercise.

__ No, I believe it's best to take a break from this exercise for awhile. I'll consider it again on _____ (target date). (You may find you can pick up where you left off. Or, start over with the second chart on page 40).

Take time now to pray, confessing your failures, praising God for your successes, and asking him for continued strength.

Chart Interpretation
After Week 6

With one more week left in this fifty-day exercise, this is a good time to evaluate your chart (page 22).

This is what's happened in the last two weeks, and why:

_____

_____

As I look at my graph for the entire six weeks, this is how I feel:

_____

As Jesus looks at my chart, this is what I sense he is saying to me:

_____

_____

It may be that as you look at the past six weeks, you are encouraged with your progress. That's wonderful! You're tasting the glorious freedom that comes with a new strength to overcome temptation.

But perhaps you have not yet enjoyed the level of success you'd hoped for when you began this exercise in reversing self-destructive patterns. Don't give up! You still have a great opportunity to see real progress! Take some time now to think about the following statement:

Here's what would have to happen for me to experience a real breakthrough before the end of these fifty days (choose one or two):

__ Ask someone to hold me accountable.

__ Increase my effort to memorize Scripture.

__ Make a serious commitment to change.

__ Set up a plan.

__ Confess my failures to God.

__ Pray more consistently about this area of my life.

__ Other: _____.

This is what makes my self-destructive pattern seem so hard to change:

_____

_____

(Note: Many self-destructive patterns are quite serious, beyond the scope of a simple fifty-day exercise. If you're fighting a problem that seems too much for you, talk to a pastor or another mature Christian. He or she may recommend a book, a support group, or even a professional counselor. The Lord can use those means to do great things.)

Wrapping Up

Your fifty-day program for reversing a self-destructive pattern is now over. Perhaps you've made significant progress. We hope you have! If so, some sort of celebration is in order. Here are some ways you could mark this milestone in your life.

• Note this accomplishment in your Bible or prayer journal.

• Contribute flowers or a plant for your Sunday worship service. Let these symbols of new life remind you of the spiritual growth you've experienced through this discipline.

• Frame one of the Scripture verses you memorized. Hang it where you'll see it often and remember the victory God gave you.

• Buy a new scarf or tie. Whenever you wear it, remember how God helped you overcome your temptation.

• Celebrate with a friend by having a meal together, going to a special event, etc.

Here's how I plan to celebrate my progress:

_____

_____

On the other hand, perhaps you haven't been as successful at resisting your temptation as you wanted to be. If that's the case, you may have tried to do this exercise on your own, without any outside encouragement. Did you go beyond the "privacy barrier"?

I asked another person to check on my progress.

__ Yes __ No

You may decide to continue working on your self-destructive pattern for another fifty days. Or, you may be ready to tackle another problem. Why not use the process you've learned through this exercise? A fresh set of charts and evaluation tools begins on page 36.

If you've seen God work in a special way through this exercise, what does that show you about the power of Christ in your life?

_____

_____

Concluding Thoughts

To bring closure to this fifty-day exercise, take a few moments to write down some of your feelings about the experience. You might use what you write as a kind of script to tell someone else about your venture. Or, share your feelings with the authors at "The Chapel of the Air." Write us at Box 30, Wheaton, Illinois 60189-0030.

Second Fifty-Day Exercise

Would you like more practice in reversing the self-destructive pattern you've been working on? Or perhaps you're ready to tackle a different self-destructive behavior. On the pages that follow, you'll find a fresh chart, weekly checkpoints, and chart interpretation questions to take you through another fifty days. But before you begin, it will be helpful to review the six steps of the Game Plan.

1. Identify a self-destructive pattern.

What are some temptations that continually trouble you? Ask the Holy Spirit to help you pinpoint a behavior pattern he wants to change in you. If you feel comfortable doing so, write on this line the self-destructive pattern you will be seeking to reverse during these fifty days:

_____

On page 10, you listed some personal benefits you would enjoy if you could resist a particular temptation. Now think about the self-destructive pattern you will be working on for the next fifty days. What will be the advantages of reversing this habit?

1.

2.

3.

4.

5.

2. Chart your behavior.

Each day, ask Jesus how he would rate your progress on a scale of 1 to 10 (10 means you are successfully overcoming the temptation and saying no to this self-destructive behavior). Then mark that point on the chart on page 40. There is a vertical line for each day; put a dot at the proper 1-10 level. As you connect the dots, you will see a pattern emerge. If you don't encounter your temptation, just skip that day on your chart. You can still connect the dots.

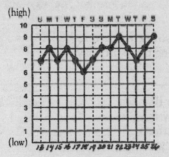

It's helpful to picture what victory over your self-destructive pattern will be like. What specific behaviors might mark your day when Jesus gives you a rating of 10?

_____

_____

_____

3. Analyze the pattern.

Special questions are included to help you interpret your chart after Weeks 2, 4, and 6 (see pages 43-51). You will be analyzing not only the timing of any sudden falls, but also the surrounding circumstances, who you were with, and so on.

4. Plan new behavior strategies.

You will use your analysis to plan new ways of living that should help you say no to this temptation more successfully. For instance, Jack is trying to change a pattern of insulting his wife. He discovers that he's especially nasty to her after he's been around his old buddy Frank. One way Jack can start to overcome his sin is to spend less time with Frank. Not all strategies will be that simple, but you should find specific ways to plan for improvement.

5. Memorize Scripture.

During the course of these fifty days, we suggest four passages that you will find especially helpful as you encounter temptation. They're listed under the "Weekly Checkpoints" on pages 41-42. Memorize these verses. Arm yourself with them. Use them. If you need help in how to go about memorizing verses, see the suggestions listed on page 57-59.

We also ask you to find and memorize three short passages that relate specifically to your particular self-destructive pattern. If you want suggestions, Part 3 of this book lists verses on thirty common temptations. Note the verses you choose on the "Weekly Checkpoints" page.

6. Tell someone that you're doing this exercise.

It's always best if you can be completely honest, but it's not absolutely necessary to reveal the specific temptation you're confronting. At least tell the person that you're working on a problem area and would like him or her to check on your progress.

Remember: As you seek to imitate Christ, "it is God who works in you to will and to act according to his good purpose."

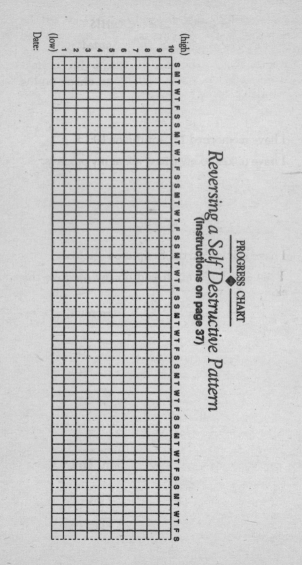

PROGRESS CHART

Reversing a Self Destructive Pattern
(instructions on page 37)

(high)

10
9
8
7
6
5
4
3
2
1

(low)

Date:

S M T W T F S S M T W T F S S M T W T F S S M T W T F S S M T W T F S S M T W T F S S M T W T F S S M T W T F S S M T W T F S S M T W T F S

Weekly Checkpoints

Preparation Step to Get Started

__ I have told a friend that I'm doing this fifty-day exercise, and I've asked him/her to check on my progress each week.

Week 1

__ I have memorized 1 Corinthians 10:13.

__ I have talked to my friend about my progress.

Week 2

__ I have chosen a Scripture to memorize related to my particular self-destructive pattern. The Scripture is _____.

__ I have memorized the Scripture I selected.

__ I have updated my friend on my progress this week.

__ I have completed the chart interpretation questions on pages 43-46.

Week 3

__ I have memorized Genesis 4:7.

__ I have updated my friend on my progress this week.

Week 4

__ I have chosen a Scripture to memorize related to my particular self-destructive pattern. The Scripture is _____.

__ I have memorized the Scripture I selected.

__ I have updated my friend on my progress this week.

__ I have completed the chart interpretation questions on pages 47-49.

Week 5

__ I have memorized Hebrews 4:15, 16.

__ I have updated my friend on my progress this week.

Week 6

__ I have chosen a Scripture to memorize related to my particular self-destructive pattern. The Scripture is _____.

__ I have memorized the Scripture I selected.

__ I have updated my friend on my progress this week.

__ I have completed the chart interpretation questions on pages 50-51.

Week 7

__ I have memorized Philippians 4:8.

__ I have updated my friend on my progress this week.

__ I have followed the suggestions on page 52 to bring closure to this fifty-day exercise.

Chart Interpretation
After Week 2

Look at the chart you've kept over the last two weeks (page 00). Maybe you're extremely pleased with your progress—that's great!

Now it's time to interpret your graph. Here are a few examples.

If your chart looks like this, you do well on the weekends but have trouble during the week:

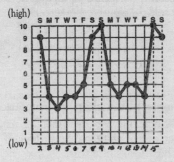

In contrast, if your chart looks like this, your trouble spots occur on the weekends:

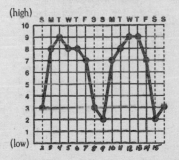

Perhaps you memorized the Scripture for the first week but let the second week's memory work slide. That may have affected your progress so that your chart looks like this:

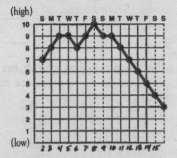

Maybe you were doing very well until, suddenly and unexpectedly, something tripped you. You thought, *If I can't get a perfect score, I might as well give up*. Your defeat lasted several days. If that's the case, your chart looks like this:

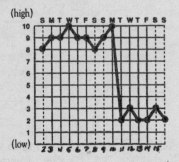

Whatever your chart looks like, this may be the first time you've ever seen your response to this temptation actually pictured before your eyes. Ask

the Lord to help you interpret your graph. You may
be pleased; you may be disturbed.

This is what my chart tells me about my progress
in reversing my self-destructive pattern:

_____

_____

I have asked someone to check on how I'm
doing. I think it would be appropriate to ask that
person to pray for me as well.

__ Yes __ No

If your chart shows a sudden upsurge or downturn, think back through the events of those days.
Were there certain people you spent time with who
may have affected your behavior in positive or
negative ways?

These people affected my progress. Here's how:

_____

_____

These circumstances or events affected my
behavior (being away from home, pressure at work,
TV programs, staying up late, being sick, etc.):

_____

_____

What can you do to avoid yielding to your temptation the next time a troublesome situation arises?

_____

_____

Here's the positive coping technique I'm planning now to replace my self-destructive response:

_____

_____

Review the benefits of being free from your self-destructive pattern that you listed on page 36. Now take time to pray about it. Ask God to forgive you for your failures. Thank him for your victories. Ask him to help you implement the strategies you've worked out. And praise him for his patience and unconditional love.

(Note: If your scores are consistently below 4, you may need to go to someone for help. Again, you could ask a spiritually minded friend to hold you accountable. Or, you might talk to a minister or Christian counselor.)

Chart Interpretation
After Week 4

Now that you've charted your progress for four weeks, you're gaining more and more perspective on reversing your self-destructive pattern. So this is a good time to stop and evaluate again.

Remember the difference between temptation and sin? As we said in the introduction, temptation in itself is not bad. Because you're currently battling a self-destructive pattern, you may find that you're being tempted more often than usual. But don't lose sight of your goal. You should be charting only your *response* to temptation.

What does your chart look like (page 40)? Do you see an upward or downward slope, or a straight horizontal line? Have you reached a plateau?

The overall pattern of my chart is _____.

Is there a specific day of the week that seems to present a special problem for me? This might be the reason:

__ It's payday.

__ I always watch a certain TV program.

__ I usually see _____ (name of person).

__ Other: _____.

This is how I would describe my feelings about overcoming my self-destructive pattern:

__ Determined

__ Still trying

__ Backing off

__ Ambivalent

__ I'm not sure I feel committed to mastering my self-destructive pattern. This is what's holding me back:

_____

_____

__ I could really use a boost to improve my progress. Here's what I need:

_____

_____

I am continuing to memorize Scripture.

__ Yes __ No

If no, here's the reason:

_____

It's possible that since the beginning of this exercise, you've received some disturbing news or experienced added tension in your life. Or it could be that you've worked so hard to overcome temptation that the matter has become obsessive. In either case, you may need to relax and let go of this venture for awhile. That's okay. Decide whether this is a healthy exercise for you to continue at this time.

__ Yes, I plan to continue this exercise.

__ No, I believe it's best to take a break from this exercise for awhile. I'll consider it again on _____ (target date). (You may find you can pick up where you left off. Or, start over with a new chart you can create yourself).

Take time now to pray, confessing your failures, praising God for your successes, and asking him for continued strength.

Chart Interpretation
After Week 6

With one more week left in this fifty-day exercise, this is a good time to evaluate your chart (page 40).

This is what's happened in the last two weeks, and why:

_____

_____

As I look at my graph for the entire six weeks, this is how I feel:

_____

As Jesus looks at my chart, this is what I sense he is saying to me:

_____

_____

It may be that as you look at the past six weeks, you are encouraged with your progress. That's wonderful! You're tasting the glorious freedom that comes with a new strength to overcome temptation.

But perhaps you have not yet enjoyed the level of success you'd hoped for when you began this exercise in reversing self-destructive patterns. Don't give up! You still have a great opportunity to see real progress! Take some time now to think about the following statement:

Here's what would have to happen for me to experience a real breakthrough before the end of these fifty days (choose one or two):

__ Ask someone to hold me accountable.

__ Increase my effort to memorize Scripture.

__ Make a serious commitment to change.

__ Set up a plan.

__ Confess my failures to God.

__ Pray more consistently about this area of my life.

__ Other: _____.

This is what makes my self-destructive pattern seem so hard to change:

_____ _____

_____

(Note: Many self-destructive patterns are quite serious, beyond the scope of a simple fifty-day exercise. If you're fighting a problem that seems too much for you, talk to a pastor or another mature Christian. He or she may recommend a book, a support group, or even a professional counselor. The Lord can use those means to do great things.)

Wrapping Up

Your fifty-day program for reversing a self-destructive pattern is now over. Perhaps you've made significant progress. We hope you have! If so, some sort of celebration is in order. Here are some ways you could mark this milestone in your life.

- Note this accomplishment in your Bible or prayer journal.

- Contribute flowers or a plant for your Sunday worship service. Let these symbols of new life remind you of the spiritual growth you've experienced through this discipline.

- Frame one of the Scripture verses you memorized. Hang it where you'll see it often and remember the victory God gave you.

- Buy a new scarf or tie. Whenever you wear it, remember how God helped you overcome your temptation.

- Celebrate with a friend by having a meal together, going to a special event, etc.

Here's how I plan to celebrate my progress:

_____

_____

On the other hand, perhaps you haven't been as successful at resisting your temptation as you wanted to be. If that's the case, you may have tried to do this exercise on your own, without any outside encouragement. Did you go beyond the "privacy barrier"?

I asked another person to check on my progress.

__ Yes   __ No

You may decide to continue working on your self-destructive pattern for another fifty days. Or, you may be ready to tackle another problem. Why not use the process you've learned through this exercise? Feel free to copy the charts and evaluation tools in this book.

If you've seen God work in a special way through this exercise, what does that show you about the power of Christ in your life?

_____

_____

Concluding Thoughts

To bring closure to this fifty-day exercise, take a few moments to write down some of your feelings about the experience. You might use what you write as a kind of script to tell someone else about your venture. Or, share your feelings with the authors at "The Chapel of the Air." Write us at Box 30, Wheaton, Illinois 60189-0030.

Part 3
Common Self-Destructive Patterns

Tips for Memorizing Scripture

A story is told of Albert Einstein, the "father of the atomic age." While in New York to make a speech, he got lost after forgetting the name of his hotel. It's reassuring that even one of the greatest minds of this century occasionally had problems with memory.

Most of us would like to improve our ability to memorize and retain information. And what information could be more important than the truths of Scripture? But memorizing it? Well, that can sometimes be a problem.

Here are some mnemonic tips (techniques for improving the memory).

1. Study actively.

How well we perform a task is determined by how much mental energy we devote to it. Research indicates that well-learned material can be remembered for at least twenty-five years, even if it is never used or rehearsed!

George Bell, a noted expert on memory skills, captures the needed mindset with the acronym AIM. The "A" stands for attention, "I" for interest, and "M" for motivation. Without motivation it is difficult to be interested, and without interest it is difficult to pay attention. Information memorized with high mental energy and enthusiastic interest is more likely to be retained.[2]

2. Eliminate distractions.

Wandering attention affects the ability to retain information. What has not been put into the memory can never be retrieved. Avoid outside interference, noise, anxiety, and stress when attempting to memorize.

3. Visualize the concepts being learned.

Don't just memorize words. Form mental pictures of the ideas being learned. Exaggerated and imaginative pictures form memory associations that are more easily recalled. For example, if you were memorizing John 15:1 with its image of vines, you might try visualizing vines loaded with fruit growing up and over a large number 1 (to represent the verse number). The more detailed and exaggerated the imagery, the easier the recall will be.

4. Remembering the context helps you retrieve information.

For example, if you learn certain verses while riding a train or waiting for a doctor's appointment, associate that setting with the verse. The linkage of the two will help when you are trying to recall the memorized information.

5. Acknowledge your limitations.

Studies show that both children and adults tire after half an hour of concentrated memorizing. So start small. Spend just a few minutes learning Scripture each day. You might go longer if you can, but keep in mind that after thirty minutes you could experience frustration and decreased productivity.

6. Repetition is necessary for retention.

Memorizing is a skill that gets better with practice. One good method is to print Scripture on easy-to-carry three-by-five cards, which you can review during your spare time. Another technique is to go over the material with another person or with a practice tape that you can make on your own. We've found that a practice tape is a great boost to memorizing. You can use it in the car or at home, and it really speeds up the memory process. You might even put the Scripture to music or find a hymn or chorus based on the verses you're learning.

7. *Accountability is a great motivator.*

Education is built on the principle of accountability. When a test or quiz is on the horizon, most students become more serious about conquering assigned material. So invite another person to memorize with you, and set specific deadlines. Or give another person the right to hold you accountable in this area. Ask him or her to check on your progress.

8. *A final word of encouragement.*

When confidence wanes and you doubt your ability to master the material, remember this fact: If you stored ten bits of information every second of your life, by your one hundredth birthday you would have used up far less than half the storage capacity of your brain.[3] Don't give up! You can do it!

Abusive Behavior

"If it makes you nervous to have someone my size in your face," says 7' 4" Mark Eaton of the NBA's Utah Jazz as he glares out from the television ad, "now you know how your kid feels when you're in his." Unfortunately, kids aren't the only victims of abusive behavior—look around and you'll see abused wives, abused elderly parents, abused people of all ages and backgrounds. But people are made in God's image . . . and how we treat them shows what we think of God.

As for the deeds of men—by the word of your lips I have kept myself from the ways of the violent (Psalm 17:4).

Do not envy a violent man or choose any of his ways, for the LORD detests a perverse man but takes the upright into his confidence (Proverbs 3:31, 32).

Even though I was once a blasphemer and a persecutor and a violent man, I was shown mercy because I acted in ignorance and unbelief. . . . . Here is a trustworthy saying that deserves full acceptance: Christ Jesus came into the world to save sinners—of whom I am the worst (1 Timothy 1:13, 15).

Since an overseer is entrusted with God's work, he must be blameless—not overbearing, not quick-tempered, not given to drunkenness, not violent, not pursuing dishonest gain. Rather he must be hospitable, one who loves what is good, who is self-controlled, upright, holy and disciplined (Titus 1:7, 8).

Example: 2 Samuel 13:1-22

Addictions

Just one more puff on the cigarette. Just one last snort of cocaine. Just one more bet on the horses. Just one last drink before you go. Just one more, just one more, just one more. . . . But it's never just one more. You're hooked, addicted, a slave to something you thought sure you could control. By now you know you were wrong. And it's time you did something about it—before you're *dead* wrong.

Do not offer the parts of your body to sin, as instruments of wickedness, but rather offer yourselves to God, as those who have been brought from death to life; and offer the parts of your body to him as instruments of righteousness. For sin shall not be your master, because you are not under law, but under grace (Romans 6:12-14).

Therefore, I urge you, brothers, in view of God's mercy, to offer your bodies as living sacrifices, holy and pleasing to God—this is your spiritual act of worship. Do not conform any longer to the pattern of this world, but be transformed by the renewing of your mind. Then you will be able to test and approve what God's will is—his good, pleasing and perfect will (Romans 12:1, 2).

Do you not know that your body is a temple of the Holy Spirit, who is in you, whom you have received from God? You are not your own; you were bought at a price. Therefore honor God with your body (1 Corinthians 6:19, 20).

Do not get drunk on wine, which leads to debauchery. Instead, be filled with the Spirit (Ephesians 5:18).

Examples: Philippians 3:18-21; Proverbs 23:29-32

Arrogance

If there's one self-destructive pattern that we detest in others but rarely detect in ourselves, it's this one. We think we're merely reporting the facts; others call it boasting. We believe we carry ourselves with dignity; others think we're haughty. We consider ourselves confident; others label us cocky. If it's true that arrogance is what transformed a glorious angel into Satan, what makes us think it won't affect us as well?

Before his downfall a man's heart is proud, but humility comes before honor (Proverbs 18:12).

Let another praise you, and not your own mouth; someone else, and not your own lips (Proverbs 27:2).

This is what the LORD says: "Let not the wise man boast of his wisdom or the strong man boast of his strength or the rich man boast of his riches, but let him who boasts boast about this: that he understands and knows me, that I am the LORD, who exercises kindness, justice and righteousness on earth, for in these I delight," declares the LORD (Jeremiah 9:23, 24).

Young men, in the same way be submissive to those who are older. All of you, clothe yourselves with humility toward one another, because, "God opposes the proud but gives grace to the humble." Humble yourselves, therefore, under God's mighty hand, that he may lift you up in due time (1 Peter 5:5-6).

Example: James 4:13-16

Breaking Promises

"His promise is as good as gold"—you don't hear that phrase much today, do you? We live in a world where broken promises are as common as dandelions (and just as noxious). God says that when we give our word, we are to keep it. How are you doing on this score?

When a man makes a vow to the LORD or takes an oath to obligate himself by a pledge, he must not break his word but must do everything he said (Numbers 30:2).

If you make a vow to the LORD your God, do not be slow to pay it, for the LORD your God will certainly demand it of you and you will be guilty of sin. . . . Whatever your lips utter you must be sure to do, because you made your vow freely to the LORD your God with your own mouth (Deuteronomy 23:21, 23).

LORD, who may dwell in your sanctuary? Who may live on your holy hill? He whose walk is blameless and who does what is righteous, who speaks the truth from his heart . . . who keeps his oath even when it hurts . . . (Psalm 15:1, 2, 4).

It is better not to vow than to make a vow and not fulfill it. Do not let your mouth lead you into sin. And do not protest . . . "My vow was a mistake." Why should God be angry at what you say and destroy the work of your hands? (Ecclesiastes 5:5, 6).

Example: Nehemiah 5:1-13

Critical Spirit

The boss can't do anything right. The pastor smiles too much. The salesperson's cologne reeks. The pianist obviously never studied music theory. The choir always sings off-key. The mailman, the clerk, the typist, the mayor, the reporter, you name it—they're all incompetent. Hear yourself in any of these comments? If so, you've got an ugly case of Critical Spirit, and the Chief Physician has just the medicine for you.

With his mouth the godless destroys his neighbor, but through knowledge the righteous escape (Proverbs 11:9).

"Do not judge, or you too will be judged. For in the same way you judge others, you will be judged, and with the measure you use, it will be measured to you" (Matthew 7:1, 2).

Therefore let us stop passing judgment on one another. Instead, make up your mind not to put any stumbling block or obstacle in your brother's way. . . . Let us therefore make every effort to do what leads to peace and to mutual edification (Romans 14:13, 19).

The entire law is summed up in a single command: "Love your neighbor as yourself." If you keep on biting and devouring each other, watch out or you will be destroyed by each other (Galatians 5:14, 15).

Do everything without complaining or arguing, so that you may become blameless and pure, children of God without fault in a crooked and depraved generation, in which you shine like stars in the universe . . . (Philippians 2:14, 15).

Examples: 1 Corinthians 10:23-33; Matthew 7:3-5

Dishonesty

Maybe it's those two-hour lunches that have been nagging at your conscience. Or perhaps it's the car you sold "in excellent condition" that you knew was about to pump its last piston. Or might the reason for your sleeplessness have something to do with not reporting that $2,000 bonus on last year's income tax return? Whatever "it" is, you know it's dishonest, and you want to change. With God's help, you can.

No one who practices deceit will dwell in my house; no one who speaks falsely will stand in my presence (Psalm 101:7).

Like a partridge that hatches eggs it did not lay is the man who gains riches by unjust means. When his life is half gone, they will desert him, and in the end he will prove to be a fool (Jeremiah 17:11).

" 'Woe to him who piles up stolen goods and makes himself wealthy by extortion! How long must this go on?' Will not your debtors suddenly arise? Will they not wake up and make you tremble? Then you will become their victim" (Habakkuk 2:6b, 7).

Therefore, rid yourselves of all malice and all deceit, hypocrisy, envy, and slander of every kind. Like newborn babies, crave pure spiritual milk, so that by it you may grow up in your salvation . . . (1 Peter 2:1, 2).

Live such good lives among the pagans that, though they accuse you of doing wrong, they may see your good deeds and glorify God on the day he visits us (1 Peter 2: 12).

Example: Acts 5:1-11

Disrespect for Authority

In a society where policemen are called "pigs" and presidents "wimps" and preachers "parasites," it's not hard to understand how disrespect for authority grows out of control. The sad truth is, however, that even Christians occasionally forget the Bible's instructions to honor those in authority—parents, employers, public officials—even when their actions are sometimes irritating.

Everyone must submit himself to the governing authorities, for there is no authority except that which God has established. The authorities that exist have been established by God. Consequently, he who rebels against the authority is rebelling against what God has instituted, and those who do so will bring judgment on themselves (Romans 13:1, 2).

Children, obey your parents in the Lord, for this is right. "Honor your father and mother"—which is the first commandment with a promise—"that it may go well with you and that you may enjoy long life on the earth" (Ephesians 6:1-3).

Now we ask you, brothers, to respect those who work hard among you, who are over you in the Lord and who admonish you. Hold them in the highest regard in love because of their work. (1 Thessalonians 5:12, 13).

Obey your leaders and submit to their authority. They keep watch over you as men who must give an account. Obey them so that their work will be a joy, not a burden, for that would be of no advantage to you (Hebrews 13:17).

Example: Numbers 16:1-50

Gossip

"Oh, you'll never believe what happened to Cheryl last night . . ." "You mean you didn't hear about Dave? Well, get a load of this . . ." Gossip. Poisoned tongues. Spreading rumors without first checking the facts. To be sure, we don't usually admit that we're gossiping. More often we claim we're just "sharing" or "making a prayer request." But that doesn't change God's attitude about it. He hates it.

There are six things the LORD hates, seven that are detestable to him: haughty eyes, a lying tongue, hands that shed innocent blood, a heart that devises wicked schemes, feet that are quick to rush into evil, a false witness who pours out lies and a man who stirs up dissension among brothers (Proverbs 6:16-19).

A perverse man stirs up dissension, and a gossip separates close friends (Proverbs 16:28).

A gossip betrays a confidence; so avoid a man who talks too much (Proverbs 20:19).

Without wood a fire goes out; without gossip a quarrel dies down. As charcoal to embers and as wood to fire, so is a quarrelsome man for kindling strife. The words of a gossip are like choice morsels; they go down to a man's inmost parts (Proverbs 26:20-22).

If anyone considers himself religious and yet does not keep a tight rein on his tongue, he deceives himself and his religion is worthless (James 1:26).

Example: 3 John 9-11

Holding a Grudge

It may have been years since Heather made that cutting remark about your weight at the office Christmas party, but you haven't forgotten. You've forgiven her, of course—Jesus said we had to—but you're not about to forget! And as your bitterness grows, your spirit shrinks. Before you know it, there's no "you" left at all . . . just a dry, cracked shell that answers whenever your name is called.

" 'Do not seek revenge or bear a grudge against one of your people, but love your neighbor as yourself. I am the LORD' " (Leviticus 19:18).

Love is patient, love is kind. It does not envy, it does not boast, it is not proud. It is not rude, it is not self-seeking, it is not easily angered, it keeps no record of wrongs. Love does not delight in evil but rejoices with the truth (1 Corinthians 13:4-6).

Bear with each other and forgive whatever grievances you may have against one another. Forgive as the Lord forgave you (Colossians 3:13).

Finally, all of you, live in harmony with one another; be sympathetic, love as brothers, be compassionate and humble. Do not repay evil with evil or insult with insult, but with blessing, because to this you were called so that you may inherit a blessing (1 Peter 3:8, 9).

See to it that no one misses the grace of God and that no bitter root grows up to cause trouble and defile many (Hebrews 12:15).

Example: Genesis 27:1-45

Illicit Sex

It's hard to live in a culture that glorifies and worships sex without allowing those self-destructive attitudes to seep into our own thinking. But the Bible makes it clear: Sex outside of marriage is wrong, every time. If we disregard God's warnings, we only ensure our own downfall.

For these commands are a lamp, this teaching is a light, and the corrections of discipline are the way to life, keeping you from the immoral woman, from the smooth tongue of the wayward wife. Do not lust in your heart after her beauty or let her captivate you with her eyes, for the prostitute reduces you to a loaf of bread, and the adulteress preys upon your very life (Proverbs 6:23-26).

Do you not know that the wicked will not inherit the kingdom of God? Do not be deceived: Neither the sexually immoral nor idolaters nor adulterers nor male prostitutes nor homosexual offenders nor thieves nor the greedy nor drunkards nor slanderers nor swindlers will inherit the kingdom of God (1 Corinthians 6:9-10).

Flee from sexual immorality. All other sins a man commits are outside his body, but he who sins sexually sins against his own body (1 Corinthians 6:18).

It is God's will that you should be sanctified: that you should avoid sexual immorality (1 Thessalonians 4:3).

Marriage should be honored by all, and the marriage bed kept pure, for God will judge the adulterer and all the sexually immoral (Hebrews 13:4).

Example: 1 Corinthians 5:1-5

Inflexibility

Rock solid is a nice thing to be for tanks and armored personnel carriers, but it's a lousy way to move through life. Inflexible people who won't budge an inch make life tough on everyone. There's not much difference between the playground wail of "We do it my way or I take home my soccer ball," and the adult who says, "We've never done it like that before, and we're not starting now." Give-and-take is part of what the Bible means by Christlikeness.

I will instruct you and teach you in the way you should go; I will counsel you and watch over you. Do not be like the horse or the mule, which have no understanding but must be controlled by bit and bridle or they will not come to you (Psalm 32:8, 9).

Trust in the LORD with all your heart and lean not on your own understanding; in all your ways acknowledge him, and he will make your paths straight. Do not be wise in your own eyes; fear the LORD and shun evil (Proverbs 3:5-7).

An unfriendly man pursues selfish ends; he defies all sound judgment. A fool finds no pleasure in understanding but delights in airing his own opinions (Proverbs 18:1, 2).

A man who remains stiff-necked after many rebukes will suddenly be destroyed—without remedy (Proverbs 29:1).

Example: Zechariah 7:8-14

Jealousy/Envy

He's never yet made it into a horror film, but he's one of the most vicious brutes around . . . Jealousy, the Green-Eyed Monster. He's killed more relationships than Hollywood has concocted. Often he gets help from his cousin, Envy, the Yellow-Eyed Monster. Together, these two roam the planet for folks who aren't content with what they have.

You shall not covet your neighbor's house. You shall not covet your neighbor's wife, or his manservant or maidservant, his ox or donkey, or anything that belongs to your neighbor (Exodus 20:17).

Do not be overawed when a man grows rich, when the splendor of his house increases; for he will take nothing with him when he dies, his splendor will not descend with him (Psalm 49:16-17).

A heart at peace gives life to the body, but envy rots the bones (Proverbs 14:30).

Do not let your heart envy sinners, but always be zealous for the fear of the LORD (Proverbs 23:17).

Anger is cruel and fury overwhelming, but who can stand before jealousy? (Proverbs 27:4).

Since we live by the Spirit, let us keep in step with the Spirit. Let us not become conceited, provoking and envying each other (Galatians 5:25, 26).

But if you harbor bitter envy and selfish ambition in your hearts, do not boast about it or deny the truth. . . . For where you have envy and selfish ambition, there you find disorder and every evil practice (James 3:14, 16).

Example: 1 Samuel 18:1-12

Lust

How much harm can a little fantasy cause? The answer many folks give is, "Not much," as they picture themselves in a passionate embrace with a friend, co-worker, or stranger. They forget that adultery doesn't start when you take off your clothes to lie naked in bed with a man or woman who isn't your spouse; adultery starts in the mind when you let your imagination take you places you were never meant to be.

"You have heard that it was said, 'Do not commit adultery.' But I tell you that anyone who looks at a woman lustfully has already committed adultery with her in his heart" (Matthew 5:27-28).

Put to death, therefore, whatever belongs to your earthly nature: sexual immorality, impurity, lust, evil desires and greed, which is idolatry. Because of these, the wrath of God is coming (Colossians 3:5-6).

It is God's will that you should be sanctified: that you should avoid sexual immorality; that each of you should learn to control his own body in a way that is holy and honorable, not in passionate lust like the heathen, who do not know God (1 Thessalonians 4:3-5).

Do not love the world or anything in the world. If anyone loves the world, the love of the Father is not in him. For everything in the world—the cravings of sinful man, the lust of his eyes and the boasting of what he has and does—comes not from the Father but from the world (1 John 2:15, 16).

Example: 2 Samuel 11:1-27

Lying

The term "little white lie" may be one of the biggest frauds ever perpetrated on humankind. The fact is, there is no such thing. A little lie is no different from a big one; a lie is a lie is a lie. Whether it's an exaggeration meant to impress, a half-truth meant to cover up, a deception meant to defraud, or a bald-faced whopper meant to destroy, we sin whenever we only pretend to tell the truth.

Truthful lips endure forever, but a lying tongue lasts only a moment. The LORD detests lying lips, but he delights in men who are truthful (Proverbs 12:19,22).

A false witness will not go unpunished, and he who pours out lies will not go free (Proverbs 19:5).

A lying tongue hates those it hurts, and a flattering mouth works ruin (Proverbs 26:28).

Therefore each of you must put off falsehood and speak truthfully to his neighbor, for we are all members of one body (Ephesians 4:25).

Do not lie to each other, since you have taken off your old self with its practices and have put on the new self, which is being renewed in knowledge in the image of its Creator (Colossians 3:9, 10).

Example: Proverbs 6:16-19

Materialism

In two hundred years, every Mercedes now on the road will be scrap (the same as every Hyundai). Every Rolex will be junk, every cellular phone a museum piece, every $350 designer shirt dust. So why is it we spend so much time worrying about such things? It's okay for kids to pretend, but why do we adults spend so much time in this imaginary world? The Bible shows how to leave this Never-Never Land to Peter Pan and his ilk.

Whoever loves money never has money enough; whoever loves wealth is never satisfied with his income. This too is meaningless (Ecclesiastes 5:10).

Do not store up for yourselves treasures on earth, where moth and rust destroy, and where thieves break in and steal. But store up for yourselves treasures in heaven, where moth and rust do not destroy, and where thieves do not break in and steal. For where your treasure is, there your heart will be also (Matthew 6:19-21).

No one can serve two masters. Either he will hate the one and love the other, or he will be devoted to the one and despise the other. You cannot serve both God and Money (Matthew 6:24).

People who want to get rich fall into temptation and a trap and into many foolish and harmful desires that plunge men into ruin and destruction. For the love of money is a root of all kinds of evil. Some people, eager for money, have wandered from the faith and pierced themselves with many griefs (1 Timothy 6:9, 10).

Example: Luke 12:15-21

Need to Control

Sometimes it goes under the guise of ladder-climbing. At others, it appears as one-upmanship. And at still other times it reveals itself for what it is—a power-hungry, club-wielding, button-pushing need to control. It can happen on the job, in the home, at church (committees are favorite nesting places), or anywhere. The desire for power, to lord it over another, is a deadly temptation. It must be resisted.

Also a dispute arose among them as to which of them was considered to be greatest. Jesus said to them, "The kings of the Gentiles lord it over them; and those who exercise authority over them call themselves Benefactors. But you are not to be like that. Instead, the greatest among you should be like the youngest, and the one who rules like the one who serves"(Luke 22:24-26).

Be devoted to one another in brotherly love. Honor one another above yourselves (Romans 12:10).

Do nothing out of selfish ambition or vain conceit, but in humility consider others better than yourselves (Philippians 2:3).

Make it your ambition to lead a quiet life, to mind your own business and to work with your hands, just as we told you, so that your daily life may win the respect of outsiders and so that you will not be dependent on anybody (1 Thessalonians 4:11, 12).

Example: Matthew 20:20-28

Occultism

It all seemed so innocent—a fascination with your horoscope, a round with the Ouija board, a trip to the New Age bookstore, a visit with a channeler. The sense of power you gained from your introduction to this mysterious world seemed so exciting. But "innocent" is not the word you'd choose today. You're losing your grip, and you don't know why. The Bible knows. It tells us to beware the occult and gives us the help we need to escape its dark clutches.

Let no one be found among you who sacrifices his son or daughter in the fire, who practices divination or sorcery, interprets omens, engages in witchcraft, or casts spells, or who is a medium or spiritist or who consults the dead. Anyone who does these things is detestable to the LORD . . . (Deuteronomy 18:10-13).

When men tell you to consult mediums and spiritists, who whisper and mutter, should not a people inquire of their God? Why consult the dead on behalf of the living? (Isaiah 8:19).

For our struggle is not against flesh and blood, but against the rulers, against the authorities, against the powers of this dark world and against the spiritual forces of evil in the heavenly realms. Therefore put on the full armor of God, so that when the day of evil comes, you may be able to stand your ground, and after you have done everything, to stand (Ephesians 6:12, 13).

Examples: 1 Samuel 28:1-25; Acts 19:11-20

Perfectionism

They expect to score 101 points out of a possible 100. They're prone to shredding their hand-knit sweater if they discover they purled once instead of twice. For them, good enough is never good enough. They're perfectionists, and unless they learn how to stop making impossible demands on themselves, they will soon drive themselves (and everyone else) crazy.

To all perfection I see a limit; but your commands are boundless (Psalm 119:96).

She did what she could (Mark 14:8).

But he said to me, "My grace is sufficient for you, for my power is made perfect in weakness." Therefore I will boast all the more gladly about my weaknesses, so that Christ's power may rest on me. . . . For when I am weak, then I am strong (2 Corinthians 12:9, 10b).

For it is by grace you have been saved, through faith—and this not from yourselves, it is the gift of God—not by works, so that no one can boast. For we are God's workmanship, created in Christ Jesus to do good works, which God prepared in advance for us to do (Ephesians 2:8-10).

For it is God who works in you to will and to act according to his good purpose (Philippians 2:13).

Example: Philippians 3:4b-11

Pornography

You're walking past the newsstand when you see "The Girls [or Boys] of the Southwest Conference!" leering out at you from the cover of a pornographic magazine. So you stop and look—what's the harm? "I look, I don't touch," you say to yourself. But pornography makes no such promise. For too many men and women, these lurid photos send the deceived down a long, dark alley that dead-ends in frustration.

I made a covenant with my eyes not to look lustfully at a girl (Job 31:1).

Do not lust in your heart after her beauty or let her captivate you with her eyes, for the prostitute reduces you to a loaf of bread, and the adulteress preys upon your very life. Can a man scoop fire into his lap without his clothes being burned? Can a man walk on hot coals without his feet being scorched? (Proverbs 6:25-28).

Finally, brothers, whatever is true, whatever is noble, whatever is right, whatever is pure, whatever is lovely, whatever is admirable—if anything is excellent or praiseworthy—think about such things (Philippians 4:8).

Do not love the world or anything in the world. If anyone loves the world, the love of the Father is not in him. For everything in the world—the cravings of sinful man, the lust of his eyes and the boasting of what he has and does—comes not from the Father but from the world (1 John 2:15, 16).

Example: Proverbs 7:1-27

Prayerlessness

It's an easy habit to slip into—you know you should take a few moments to pray, but you just don't see how you can spare the time right now. So you put it off until tomorrow . . . but tomorrow never comes. And soon life's troubles threaten to engulf you. It didn't need to happen! God waits to hear from us, and he's only a prayer away.

I love the LORD, for he heard my voice; he heard my cry for mercy. Because he turned his ear to me, I will call on him as long as I live (Psalm 116:1-2).

" 'Call to me and I will answer you and tell you great and unsearchable things you do not know' " (Jeremiah 33:3).

Be joyful in hope, patient in affliction, faithful in prayer (Romans 12:12).

And pray in the Spirit on all occasions with all kinds of prayers and requests. With this in mind, be alert and always keep on praying for all the saints (Ephesians 6:18)

Devote yourselves to prayer, being watchful and thankful (Colossians 4:2).

Therefore confess your sins to each other and pray for each other so that you may be healed. The prayer of a righteous man is powerful and effective (James 5:16).

Examples: 1 Samuel 12:19-23; Daniel 6:1-28

Prejudice

Archie Bunker hasn't been on prime-time television for well over a decade, but people still remember him. Who can forget his outrageous attacks against blacks, against Jews, against women or Poles or priests or anyone unlike him? Could it be we remember him so well because he reminds us of *us*? Prejudice did not die out when "All in the Family" was canceled. The only one who can cancel it in your own life is you.

Stop judging by mere appearances, and make a right judgment (John 7:24).

Live in harmony with one another. Do not be proud, but be willing to associate with people of low position. Do not be conceited (Romans 12:16).

You are all sons of God through faith in Christ Jesus, for all of you who were baptized into Christ have clothed yourselves with Christ. There is neither Jew nor Greek, slave nor free, male nor female, for you are all one in Christ Jesus (Galatians 3:26-28).

Here there is no Greek or Jew, circumcised or uncircumcised, barbarian, Scythian, slave or free, but Christ is all, and is in all (Colossians 3:11).

If you really keep the royal law found in Scripture, "Love your neighbor as yourself," you are doing right. But if you show favoritism, you sin and are convicted by the law as lawbreakers (James 2:8, 9).

Examples: James 2:1-10; Luke 10:25-37

Preoccupation with Self

The first person singular is the pronoun of preference for many of us: "I," "Me," "Mine." How easy it is to get so wrapped up in *my* plans, *my* wants, *my* schedule, *my* toys, *my* needs, *my* perspective! But unless we work to free ourselves from that kind of egocentric attitude, it won't be long before we find ourselves in an escape-proof prison that we ourselves designed and built.

Then he said to them all: "If anyone would come after me, he must deny himself and take up his cross daily and follow me. For whoever wants to save his life will lose it, but whoever loses his life for me will save it. What good is it for a man to gain the whole world, and yet lose or forfeit his very self?" (Luke 9:23-25).

For by the grace given me I say to every one of you: Do not think of yourself more highly than you ought, but rather think of yourself with sober judgment, in accordance with the measure of faith God has given you (Romans 12:3).

We who are strong ought to bear with the failings of the weak and not to please ourselves. Each of us should please his neighbor for his good, to build him up. For even Christ did not please himself . . . (Romans 15:1-3a).

I have been crucified with Christ and I no longer live, but Christ lives in me. The life I live in the body, I live by faith in the Son of God, who loved me and gave himself for me (Galatians 2:20).

Each of you should look not only to your own interests, but also to the interests of others (Philippians 2:4).
Example: Daniel 4:1-37

Procrastination

You know the dog needs a bath, but hey, "Star Trek" is on. Can't the dog wait? And yes, you're aware that the rain gutters are clogged, but look, summer's only a month away. Your favorite foreign word is "mañana" and your motto is, "Why do today what you can put off till tomorrow?" The truth is, you're a procrastinator. And lately it's gotten you into trouble (or you can see it coming). The good news is, you can do something about it.

Do not withhold good from those who deserve it, when it is in your power to act. Do not say to your neighbor, "Come back later; I'll give it tomorrow"— when you now have it with you (Proverbs 3:27, 28).

One who is slack in his work is brother to one who destroys (Proverbs 18:9).

A sluggard does not plow in season; so at harvest time he looks but finds nothing (Proverbs 20:4).

No discipline seems pleasant at the time, but painful. Later on, however, it produces a harvest of righteousness and peace for those who have been trained by it (Hebrews 12:11).

Anyone, then, who knows the good he ought to do and doesn't do it, sins (James 4:17).

Example: Luke 9:57-62

Profanity

We hear it so much nowadays that a lot goes by without our even taking notice. That's bad enough, but when the verbal raunch starts coming out of our mouth and not just into our ears, we've got a major problem. None of us are off the hook just because we don't "take the Lord's name in vain." There's a whole class of communication that the Bible strongly advises us to avoid.

You shall not misuse the name of the LORD your God, for the LORD will not hold anyone guiltless who misuses his name (Exodus 20:7).

Hear, O LORD, my righteous plea; listen to my cry. Give ear to my prayer—it does not rise from deceitful lips. . . . Though you probe my heart and examine me at night, though you test me, you will find nothing; I have resolved that my mouth will not sin (Psalm 17:1, 3).

Do not let any unwholesome talk come out of your mouths, but only what is helpful for building others up according to their needs, that it may benefit those who listen. . . . Nor should there be obscenity, foolish talk or coarse joking, which are out of place, but rather thanksgiving (Ephesians 4:29; 5:4).

With the tongue we praise our Lord and Father, and with it we curse men, who have been made in God's likeness. Out of the same mouth come praise and cursing. My brothers, this should not be (James 3:9, 10).

Example: Mark 14:66-72

Stealing

You don't need a mask and a gun in order to become a thief. You join this Fraternity of Felons every time you deliberately cheat people out of what is rightfully theirs . . . every time you take credit for what someone else accomplished . . . every time you pocket some little trinket at the store. We steal whenever we take possession of what belongs to someone else, whether it's time, money, affection, or things.

. . . give me neither poverty nor riches, but give me only my daily bread. Otherwise, I may have too much and disown you and say, "Who is the LORD?" Or I may become poor and steal, and so dishonor the name of my God (Proverbs 30:8, 9).

" 'Woe to him who piles up stolen goods and makes himself wealthy by extortion! How long must this go on?' Will not your debtors suddenly arise? Will they not wake up and make you tremble? Then you will become their victim" (Habakkuk 2:6b, 7).

"Will a man rob God? Yet you rob me. But you ask, 'How do we rob you?' In tithes and offerings . . . " (Malachi 3:8).

He who has been stealing must steal no longer, but must work, doing something useful with his own hands, that he may have something to share with those in need (Ephesians 4:28).

Example: Joshua 7:1-26

Short Temper

Snap, crackle, pop! No, that's not a popular breakfast cereal you hear, but the sound of a quick temper once again about to explode. Sometimes such an outburst only reveals the tip of the iceberg—bobbing beneath the surface is a huge, festering mountain of resentment and unresolved rage. Those who flare often—and suddenly—must deal with their anger before it deals with them.

Better a patient man than a warrior, a man who controls his temper than one who takes a city (Proverbs 16:32).

It is to a man's honor to avoid strife, but every fool is quick to quarrel (Proverbs 20:3).

"In your anger do not sin": Do not let the sun go down while you are still angry, and do not give the devil a foothold (Ephesians 4:26, 27).

Get rid of all bitterness, rage and anger, brawling and slander, along with every form of malice. Be kind and compassionate to one another, forgiving each other, just as in Christ God forgave you (Ephesians 4:31, 32).

My dear brothers, take note of this: Everyone should be quick to listen, slow to speak and slow to become angry, for man's anger does not bring about the righteous life that God desires (James 1:19, 20).

Example: Genesis 4:3-16

Unconcern

There's no reason to care much about some things—the color of your toothbrush, the brand of your wastebasket, the political preference of your florist. But to be Christlike, you must be concerned about the welfare (both physical and spiritual) of others. If you can look around, see people in need, and yet consistently turn your back and walk away without lifting a finger to help, Scripture says you're in danger.

If a man shuts his ears to the cry of the poor, he too will cry out and not be answered (Proverbs 21:13).

Share with God's people who are in need. Practice hospitality (Romans 12:13).

Keep on loving each other as brothers. Do not forget to entertain strangers, for by so doing some people have entertained angels without knowing it. Remember those in prison as if you were their fellow prisoners, and those who are mistreated as if you yourselves were suffering (Hebrews 13:1-3).

Religion that God our Father accepts as pure and faultless is this: to look after orphans and widows in their distress and to keep oneself from being polluted by the world (James 1:27).

If anyone has material possessions and sees his brother in need but has no pity on him, how can the love of God be in him? Dear children, let us not love with words or tongue but with actions and in truth (1 John 3:17, 18).

Example: Matthew 25:31-46

Wasting Time

Many folks who claim they don't possess a creative bone in their body are nevertheless able to stockpile a staggering collection of ways to waste time. Hours in front of the tube. Untold minutes gabbing on the telephone. Frequent naps. Weekends spent doing . . . what? Whenever we allow ourselves the "luxury" of wasting time, we invite a thief to steal a part of our lives we can never retrieve.

Diligent hands will rule, but laziness ends in slave labor (Proverbs 12:24).

I applied my heart to what I observed and learned a lesson from what I saw: A little sleep, a little slumber, a little folding of the hands to rest—and poverty will come on you like a bandit and scarcity like an armed man (Proverbs 24:32-34).

Be very careful, then, how you live—not as unwise but as wise, making the most of every opportunity, because the days are evil. Therefore do not be foolish, but understand what the Lord's will is (Ephesians 5:15-17).

Whatever you do, work at it with all your heart, as working for the Lord, not for men, since you know that you will receive an inheritance from the Lord as a reward. It is the Lord Christ you are serving (Colossians 3:23, 24).

Example: Ecclesiastes 3:1-8

Workaholism

The clock on your office wall tells you it's 9 P.M. Since you came in at five that morning and worked through lunch, that makes about sixteen hours today (same as yesterday). And still the pile on your desk screams at you! Your family will just have to count you out for supper again tomorrow night . . . right? If you let workaholism do this to you, it will strangle your marriage, your friendships, your health, even your relationship with the Lord. And you don't need that.

Moses' father-in-law replied, "What you are doing is not good. You and these people who come to you will only wear yourselves out. The work is too heavy for you; you cannot handle it alone" (Exodus 18:17, 18).

Six days do your work, but on the seventh day do not work, so that your ox and your donkey may rest and the slave born in your household, and the alien as well, may be refreshed (Exodus 23:12).

Unless the LORD builds the house, its builders labor in vain. Unless the LORD watches over the city, the watchmen stand guard in vain. In vain you rise early and stay up late, toiling for food to eat—for he grants sleep to those he loves (Psalm 127:1, 2).

"Come to me, all you who are weary and burdened, and I will give you rest. Take my yoke upon you and learn from me, for I am gentle and humble in heart, and you will find rest for your souls. For my yoke is easy and my burden is light" (Matthew 11:28-30).

Example: Exodus 18:17-27

Worry

Who hasn't known those terrifying, anxious moments when a loved one's return was long overdue . . . and yet you'd heard nothing? That will put a chill down anyone's spine. But some folks never get a respite from worry or anxiety or fear. They can't seem to stop biting their nails. The knot in their stomach never disappears. For all such folk, God's Word offers real hope.

When I am afraid, I will trust in you. In God, whose word I praise, in God I trust; I will not be afraid. What can mortal man do to me? (Psalm 56:3, 4).

So do not fear, for I am with you; do not be dismayed, for I am your God. I will strengthen you and help you; I will uphold you with my righteous right hand (Isaiah 41:10).

"For I know the plans I have for you," declares the LORD, "plans to prosper you and not to harm you, plans to give you hope and a future" (Jeremiah 29:11).

Therefore do not worry about tomorrow, for tomorrow will worry about itself. Each day has enough trouble of its own (Matthew 6:34).

Do not be anxious about anything, but in everything, by prayer and petition, with thanksgiving, present your requests to God. And the peace of God, which transcends all understanding, will guard your hearts and your minds in Christ Jesus (Philippians 4:6, 7).

Cast all your anxiety on him because he cares for you (1 Peter 5:7).

Example: Luke 12:22-31

Additional Verses

(Use this space to write down any Scriptures that you find especially helpful in the battle against self-destructive patterns.)

_____

_____

_____

_____

_____

_____

_____

_____

_____

_____

_____

_____

_____

_____

_____

_____

_____

Additional Verses

(Use this space to write down any Scriptures that you find especially helpful in the battle against self-destructive patterns.)

_____

_____

_____

_____

_____

_____

_____

_____

_____

_____

_____

_____

_____

_____

Additional Verses

(Use this space to write down any Scriptures that you find especially helpful in the battle against self-destructive patterns.)

_____

_____

_____

_____

_____

_____

_____

_____

_____

_____

_____

_____

_____

_____

_____

Additional Verses

(Use this space to write down any Scriptures that you find especially helpful in the battle against self-destructive patterns.)

_____

_____

_____

_____

_____

_____

_____

_____

_____

_____

_____

_____

_____

_____

Notes

1. Ogden Nash, "The Panther" in *The Oxford Book of American Light Verse*, ed. William Harmon (New York: Oxford University Press, 1979), p. 426.

2. Art Dworken, "Forget-me-not," in *American Way*, 9 July 1985, pp. 77-81.

3. Dworken, pp. 77-78.